The Pied Piper of Hamelin

Colette

DANCE PLAYS

INTERMEDIATE

Alison Chaplin

AUTHOR
Alison Chaplin

EDITOR
Joel Lane

ASSISTANT EDITOR
David Sandford

SERIES DESIGNER
Anna Oliwa/Heather Sanneh

DESIGNER
Mark Udall

ILLUSTRATIONS
Jennifer Fyfe

COVER ARTWORK
Jennifer Fyfe

Text © 2000 Alison Chaplin
© 2000 Scholastic Ltd

Designed using Adobe Pagemaker

Published by Scholastic Ltd,
Villiers House,
Clarendon Avenue,
Leamington Spa,
Warwickshire CV32 5PR

1 2 3 4 5 6 7 8 9 0   0 1 2 3 4 5 6 7 8 9

British Library Cataloguing-in-Publication Data: a catalogue record for this book is available from the British Library.

ISBN 0-439-01683-5

ACKNOWLEDGEMENTS

First performed in Manchester by participants on the 'Drama and Theatre Workshop' in August 1998, many thanks to them for their suggestions of script changes and enthusiastic performance!

For permission to give a performance of this play at which an admission charge is made, please contact the Editorial Department, Educational Books, Scholastic Limited, Villiers House, Clarendon Avenue, Leamington Spa, Warwickshire CV32 5PR. You do not need to seek permission if you do not charge an entry fee for the performance. Performing licences must be applied for prior to beginning rehearsals.

Fees are £10.00 per performance for a paying audience of up to 200 people and £15.00 per performance for paying audiences of 200 people or over.

Alison Chaplin is the drama consultant for the Borough of Stockport and manager of 'Arts on the Move', a company specializing in drama and theatre services. For information call 0161 881 0868.

CONTENTS LIST

INTRODUCTION

USING THIS BOOK

The aim of this *Scholastic Performance Play* is to provide teachers with the appropriate resources to read, rehearse and perform a short play. The book enables teachers and children to understand the process of interpreting scripts and the approaches needed for successful rehearsals and performances. From providing pre-rehearsal support to supplying linked reading and writing tasks, the book is structured in a way that assumes no prior knowledge of scriptwork and no previous experience of staging performances, leading all those involved through the process in easy-to-follow stages.

WORKSHOP SESSIONS

Workshop sessions are provided to help the teacher introduce the children to the concept of drama. The sessions help the children to:

- read and understand playscripts
- explore the implicit themes and issues within the play
- appreciate character development
- learn the skills required for performance.

Each session is structured to approach a different aspect of working with a playscript, using methods which are both practical and enjoyable.

PLAYSCRIPT

The **Playscript** is organized in an easy-to-follow format, complete with full stage directions and scene changes. At the beginning of each script, following the cast list, there is a set of brief character outlines that provide an indication of behavioural traits and help the children to understand how each role should be performed. Most of the plays in the *Performance Plays* series are simple to stage and require little in the way of make-up, costume or setting.

PRODUCTION SUPPORT

The **Production support** notes provide practical advice to support the teacher from the beginning to the end of the performance process, including: holding auditions; structuring rehearsals; simple and effective staging, props, costumes and make-up; and finally, presenting professional 'curtain calls'. The ideas provided have arisen from the author's own experience of directing this play, and are thus informed by a knowledge of what has worked in practice. However, they are not meant to be completely prescriptive: if teachers feel that they have the resources, time and skills to create more elaborate staging and costumes, or to approach the performance in a different way, then they should feel free to do so!

LITERACY SUPPORT

The **Literacy support** notes at the end of this book are directly linked to the requirements of the National Literacy Strategy *Framework for Teaching*. They provide suggestions for supportive tasks, organized under the headings: 'Story', 'Characters', 'Theme', 'Working with the playscript' and 'Performance-related tasks'. Again, these are not completely prescriptive; but they provide teachers with examples of how the playscript can be used to generate structured literacy work.

A FLEXIBLE RESOURCE

The unique aspect of these *Performance Plays* is that their contents can be utilised in a number of different ways: as a simple reading resource; to provide a basis for literacy tasks; to introduce children to the concept of performance drama; or to produce a full-scale school play. Readers should feel free to employ the book in any way that meets their needs. However, the most important approach for anyone using this play is to be flexible, enthusiastic and prepared to 'have a go'!

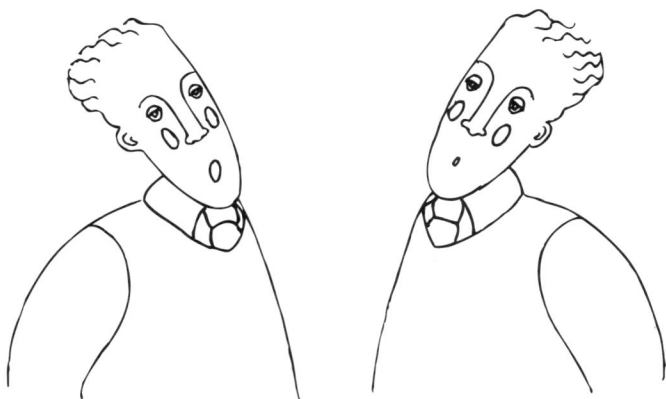

GUIDANCE FOR WORKING WITH SCRIPTS

If your children have no previous experience of script work, it is a good idea to lead them through the following simple drama process in order to make them familiar with the concept and style of a scripted performance.

Ask the children (in their classroom places) to find a partner and hold a conversation with him or her. It could be about anything: the television programmes they watched the night before, their favourite books, what they did during the school holidays, and so on. Allow these conversations to run for about a minute, then ask the children to stop talking.

Now ask the pairs to label themselves 'A' and 'B'. Tell them that they must hold a conversation again, but this time 'B' cannot respond until 'A' has finished talking (or until 'A' has finished a sentence, if 'A' is going on for too long). Insist that the children adhere to this procedure for speaking and responding, as this forms the basis for most scripted formats.

Allow these structured conversations to run for about a minute, then ask the children to stop talking. Invite them to give feedback on the type of conversations they had. Using the board, write their statements and responses in the form of an 'A said' and 'B said' structure:

A said: ....

B said: ....

Record just a couple of lines from each conversation, to show the children how these conversations can be recorded. Ask them to suggest how their second conversation was different from their first one. Answers should include: the speakers had names (as in 'A' and 'B'); they could only speak when the other person had finished speaking; the conversations were not as natural; the children had to listen more carefully and think more about what they said and how they responded to their partners.

Now ask the children to join with another pair to make a four. (Odd numbers or unequal groups are also acceptable.) Ask them to hold an initial unstructured conversation with each other on a subject of your choosing; leave these to run for about a minute. Then ask the children to label themselves 'A', 'B', 'C' and 'D' (if there are four in the group) and to hold another conversation, this time following the same restriction as before: while someone in the group is talking, no-one else can speak. Tell the children that they do not necessarily have to join in the conversation in alphabetical order.

Invite feedback about these conversations. Again, ask for comments on how the second discussion differed from the first. Record part of a structured conversation on the board, using 'A', 'B', 'C' and 'D' to indicate who speaks which lines.

Inform the children that this is how plays are structured: they are written records of people speaking to each other, having conversations or discussions; that the name of the character speaking is indicated at the beginning of each piece of dialogue.

Further practice for the children could include:

- Recording their conversations in script form, using the 'A' and 'B' or 'A', 'B', 'C', 'D' format.
- Devising and writing original conversations, using the 'A' and 'B' or 'A', 'B', 'C', 'D' format.
- Lifting a section of dialogue from a familiar story and recording it in script form.
- Rewriting their own conversations, using names instead of letters of the alphabet.
- Improvising a scene (such as someone buying an item in a shop), recording this scene using a tape recorder or dictaphone, then replaying the recording in order to write it down as a script.

The main aim is to help the children appreciate that a playscript is simply dialogue, conversations or verbal statements written down, and that the format gives a clear indication of who is speaking at any one time. Advise the children that characters may interrupt each other, but that two people will never talk at the same time during a scripted performance: the lines will always be spoken in sequence. Make sure they understand that playscripts (unlike other forms of written speech) do not contain speech marks or quotation marks, because the whole text is known and understood to be speech and so they are unnecessary.

Go on from this exercise to reading and discussing an extract from any playscript: explore how the text indicates who is speaking, analyse the sequencing of the dialogue and reaffirm the idea of characters speaking in turn.

As a final note, when reading the playscript in this book, ask the children to suggest what the purpose of the words in brackets and italics may be. They may reply: 'How characters say things', 'What characters do' or 'How characters do things'. Keep the language as simple as this initially, developing their vocabulary gradually as they become more familiar with reading and understanding scripts. (See 'Literacy support' on page 48.)

THEMES AND ISSUES IN THE PLAY

The Pied Piper of Hamelin is based on Robert Browning's poem of the same name. The play expands the text of this poem by using scripted scenes which help to explain the narrative and to link sections of the poem together. This provides the teacher with an opportunity both to explore the genre of narrative poetry and to examine a variety of issues which arise from the text of the play.

The original aim of the play was to help children appreciate how effective narrative poetry could be in describing situations and in telling an enjoyable story. The script was written in a way that made access to the poem's text easier, and children of all reading abilities were able to understand the events outlined in the story.

Central to both the poem and the play is the moral that promises should not be broken. Obviously, the Mayor's broken promise to the Pied Piper has dire consequences, which may not be quite so severe in 'real life'! However, the play supplies teachers with perfect material to stimulate discussion about the idea of making and breaking promises, providing an ideal introduction to PSHE lessons dealing with honesty and fairness.

It is also interesting to compare and contrast the characters of the Mayor and members of the council with the character of the Pied Piper, asking the children to suggest which of these they consider to be 'bad' people and why. This encourages them to reflect on their concept of 'good' and 'bad' behaviour, and the motives people may have for acting in a particular way.

The play also provides opportunities to explore the language of the poem, a mixture of Victorian and medieval English (it was written in Victorian times, but is set in 1376). It could also provide a basis for geography work: looking at the location of Hamelin and the river Weser. It could even be used to generate work on the role played by rats in causing the Black Death and the Great Plague of London.

These sessions should take place before any rehearsal or practical application of the playscript. They introduce the children to drama and theatre, develop their speaking and listening skills, increase their level of concentration, help to prepare them for the activities they will do during work on the playscript, develop their ability to perform confidently and effectively, and generate positive group interaction.

SESSION 1

INTRODUCTORY WARM-UP

Timing: Spend no more than 10 minutes on each individual activity. The whole session should take no more than 40 minutes.

Resources: a large space (such as the school hall); chairs or cushions (one per child).

Objectives: To introduce the children to the concept of drama. To encourage the children to respond appropriately to instructions. To promote positive group interaction.

FRUITBOWL

A PHYSICAL WARM-UP

Sit the children in a circle, on chairs or cushions. Go round the circle, naming each child with one of three fruit names (such as apple, orange, lemon).

Ask one child to stand in the centre of the circle. Take this child's chair or cushion away from the circle, so that you have one seat fewer than the total number of participants.

Say that when the person in the centre calls out one of the given fruit names, all the children with that name must run from their seat and try to find another. The person in the centre must also try to find a seat. You cannot return to the same chair or cushion in that turn.

Explain that since there is one chair less, someone will always be left without a seat. This person should then stand in the centre of the circle and call out another fruit name for the exchange of seats to begin again. Any of the fruit names can be called out in each turn.

Also say that if the person standing in the centre calls out 'Fruitbowl!', then everyone must swap places and try to find a new seat. Again, they cannot return to their own chairs.

The result is lots of frantic chair-swapping! Play for several turns, then go on to...

KEEP TALKING!

DEVELOPS SPEAKING AND LISTENING SKILLS

Ask the children to find a partner and a space to work in. Say that you want them to tell each other all about their day so far, from the moment they woke up this morning. They will be talking and listening to each other at the same time! The aim is to try and make your partner stop talking, while also taking in what he or she is telling you.

Ask the children to start talking to each other. Move around the room, praising those children who are concentrating on their conversations – and especially those not distracted by others or their partners.

After a short while, ask the children to stop talking. (Raise your arm in the air as a signal if they can't hear you!) Invite them to tell you about the conversations they heard, and whether they succeeded in breaking their partner's concentration.

Praise all efforts. Now ask the children to stand in a circle, and move on to...

WHO'S LEADING THE MOVEMENT?

DEVELOPS CONCENTRATION AND PROMOTES GROUP CO-OPERATION

Ask one child to leave the room, or to turn away from the rest of the group.

Silently point to another child standing in the circle. Ask this child to raise his or her hand (silently) to indicate to the others that he or she has been chosen.

Explain that you will ask this child to lead the rest of the group in making a series of simple, mimed movements. The other children must copy any movements performed by the leader, **without revealing who they are following**.

Now ask the first child to return and stand in the centre of the circle to watch as the movements are led and copied. Allow this child two or three chances to guess who's leading the movement. If the child in the centre guesses correctly, select two more children to be leader and 'guesser'. If the child can't guess who it is, the leader reveals him- or herself and two new children are chosen.

Repeat the activity two or three times. Thank the children for their efforts, and end with...

CIRCLE
CHILDREN REFLECT ON AND EVALUATE THEIR SKILLS

Ask the children to sit in a circle on the floor, on cushions or on the chairs.

Ask them whether they enjoyed the drama session or not. Ask for opinions and reasons. What do they think they have learned and achieved from it?

This gives an indication of any skills and knowledge gained, and can be used as a basis for developing children's abilities during additional sessions.

SESSION 2
APPROACHING THE TEXT

Timing: Spend up to 15 minutes on each activity. The whole session should take up to 60 minutes.
Resources: Copies of the script (one per child); groupings ready for small-group work; a board or flip chart and writing materials; a sheet of A3 paper; a marker pen.
Objective: To familiarize the children with the playscript text.

SHARED TEXT WORK
WHOLE-CLASS READING OF THE SCRIPT

Sit with the children in a circle, or in their classroom places. Distribute a copy of the playscript to each child, and retain one for yourself. If applicable, remind the children of their earlier drama exercise on understanding scripts (see page 5).

Tell the children that you are all going to read a play: *The Pied Piper of Hamelin*. Explain that you will be reading the lines for the narrators, but will choose children (or ask for volunteers) to read the lines for the other characters. Advise the children that they should **all** read and follow the words in the script while they are being read out.

Read through the script scene by scene, combining your reading with that of volunteers or nominees. At this stage, read the lines spoken only: do not mention each character name in turn, and do not read the stage directions aloud.

A possible distribution of the reading parts is as follows:

● Five children to read the lines for the MAYOR and CORPORATION 1, 2, 3 and 4 from the beginning of the play, ending on the line *Good! It appears that we are all in agreement...*
● Four children to read the lines for the four TOWNSPEOPLE from their first entrance, ending on the line *...we'll send you packing!*
● Six children to read the lines for the MAYOR, PIED PIPER and CORPORATION 1, 2, 3 and 4 from the line *For a guilder I'd my ermine gown sell...* to the end of Scene 1.
● Eight children to read the lines for the RATS during the whole of Scene 2.
● Six children to read the lines for RATS 3, 6, 4, 2, 5 and 8 during Scene 3.
● Ten children to read the lines for CHILDREN 1, 2, 3, 4, 5 and 6 and TOWNSPEOPLE 1, 2, 3 and 4 from the beginning of Scene 4, ending on the *ad lib* lines.
● Six children to read the lines for the MAYOR, PIED PIPER and CORPORATION 1, 2, 3 and 4 from the line *Go...* to the end of Scene 4.
● Six children to read the lines for CHILDREN 1, 2, 3, 4, 5 and 6 from the beginning of Scene 5, ending on the line *...Please wait for me!*
● Five children to read the lines for TOWNSPEOPLE 1, 2, 3 and 4 and CHILD 6 from the line *What's happening?...*, ending on the line *...and never hear of that country more.*
● Seven children to read the lines for TOWNSPEOPLE 1 and 2, the MAYOR and CORPORATION 1, 2, 3 and 4 from the line *What did you say to him?*, ending on the line *Neither will we, Mayor...*
● Read all of the final NARRATORS' lines yourself.

Choose your readers carefully, making sure that they are proficient enough to read the lines allocated to them, while still giving lower-ability readers the opportunity to read some lines. At the end of each reading section, thank the children for their efforts.

Finally, ask the children to turn back to the first page of their scripts. Move quickly on to...

FOCUSED WORD WORK
EXPLORING THE LANGUAGE USED IN THE PLAYSCRIPT

Invite the children to identify words from the text which they have difficulty in understanding. Specify that these must be words which they have never seen or heard before (so that they focus on learning new vocabulary). Write these words on the board or flip chart. Make sure you have sufficient space – there will probably be a great many words to record!

Work through the script quickly, recording all the children's suggestions. Use any remaining time to find definitions of as many of these words as possible. This could be achieved in a number of different ways:

- Children working in pairs or threes, using the context of the sentences to conclude what the word definitions are.
- Children working as a whole class, using the context of the sentences to conclude what the definitions are.
- Children looking the words up in a dictionary, working individually with teacher guidance.
- Children working in pairs or small groups, being allocated three or four words per pair/group and looking them up in a dictionary.
- Teacher providing the definitions on the board or flip chart.
- Teacher providing the definitions of some of the words on the board, but asking children to find the definitions of others.

The process of defining words can be made more interesting by creating teams and allocating a 'team point' each time that a word is defined correctly.

Make sure that these new words and their definitions are recorded – on paper, in spelling books, or in writing books. Leave any words still not defined for further work at a later time, and move on to...

GROUP WORK
SMALL-GROUP READINGS OF THE PLAYSCRIPT

Form the children into six groups of four to six. (It is advisable that these are of mixed reading ability.) Make sure that each child retains a copy of the playscript.

Tell the children that you want each group to read through a scene from the play, speaking the lines aloud. They have to read all of the lines spoken by the different characters in their allotted scene, and that this may mean that some children have to read more than one part. Advise them to negotiate and distribute the parts quickly and fairly, making sure that each person in their group reads at least once.

Allocate each group one of the scenes from the play. (Note that Scene 6 involves only five characters.) Move from group to group, allocating the scenes and checking that the parts have been fairly distributed.

When you have visited each group, instruct the children to start their readings. Move around the room, monitoring the readings and assisting where necessary.

Allow sufficient time for all the readings to be completed. If enough time remains, ask the groups (in sequence) to read their scene to the others.

Thank the children for their efforts. Ask them to stop reading, turn and face the board or flip chart again. Move on to...

STORY OUTLINE
WHOLE-CLASS REVIEW AND CONSOLIDATON OF KNOWLEDGE GAINED

Attach the A3 sheet of paper to the board. Write the heading 'The Pied Piper of Hamelin' on it. Invite the children to recall the story in the playscript. Do they think they could give an outline of the story in the form of a sequence of sentences describing the events?

Start them off by asking: *What is happening at the beginning of the play?* Record their answer on the A3 sheet. Now ask: *What is the next important event or moment of the play?* Continue in this fashion until you have the complete story of the play's events written on the A3 paper in the form of a sequential outline.

Take a final moment to confirm with the children that you have recorded all of the important elements of the story. Thank them for their contributions. Retain the A3 paper for use in the following session.

SESSION 3
EXPLORING THE STORYLINE

Timing: Give each activity up to 15 minutes. The whole session should take no more than 45 minutes.
Resources: A large space (such as the school hall); the A3 sheet from the previous session; chairs (optional).
Objectives: To consolidate knowledge of the play's contents. To develop drama skills.

STORYLINE FREEZES

CONSOLIDATES KNOWLEDGE OF STORYLINE AND DEVELOPS DRAMA SKILLS

Put the children into groups of five to eight. Allocate each group a sentence from the story outline recorded on the A3 sheet of paper in the previous session.

Ask each group to create a **freeze** (a still and silent picture) which represents their storyline sentence. These will then be shown, in sequence, to the rest of the group. Allow up to three minutes for the children to discuss and create their group freezes.

Nominate an area of the room to be the 'performance area'. View each freeze in sequence. Ask the 'audience' to remain silent while observing, and then to applaud each freeze viewed in turn. If time allows, follow up each freeze with a brief discussion on its composition and effectiveness.

Thank all the children for their efforts. Move on to...

STORYLINE NARRATIONS

BUILDS NARRATIVE AND PERFORMANCE SKILLS

Put the children into groups of eight to twelve. Ask them to find a space to work in.

Explain that you want each group to perform the complete story of *The Pied Piper of Hamelin*, using only **narration** (speech which explains what is happening) and **mime** (action without words or sound). The mime can be performed during the narration or after each narrative section. It must always reflect what is being (or has been) said by the narrator(s). The group can have as many narrators as they wish, but must have enough people remaining to perform the mimes.

Allow up to eight minutes for the children to discuss, plan and rehearse their performances. Move from group to group, checking that the parts have been

distributed fairly and that all the children are working productively.

When the preparation and rehearsal time has elapsed, nominate a section of the room to be the 'performance area' and view each storyline performance in turn. Each performance should take no longer than two minutes. Insist that the 'audience' remain silent while others are performing, and invite them to applaud the efforts of each group in turn.

When all of the groups have performed, invite the whole class to suggest any important elements which were omitted from any of the narrated performances. Similarly, invite positive comments on less obvious elements which were included.

Thank all the children for their efforts. Call them to sit in a circle, and move on quickly to...

THEME IMPROVISATION

EXPLORING THE MORAL OF THE PLAY

Lead a brief discussion about the central **theme** of the play, asking the children to suggest what the **moral** of the story might be. The answer might be: 'If you have made a promise to someone, you should keep it.' Acknowledge all responses.

Ask the children each to find a partner and a space to work in, and to label themselves 'A' and 'B'. Ask all those called 'A' to raise their hands, then lower them. Repeat for all those called 'B'. (For groups with an odd number of children, one pair can work as a three; or the teacher can form a pair with one of the children.)

Explain that you want the children to **improvise** a situation where 'A' has broken a promise made to 'B'. Ask them to reflect on times when they have broken promises or had promises made to them and then broken. These memories could form the basis of their improvisations.

Tell the children that they will be allowed no planning or preparation time: their dialogues must be acted out **spontaneously**. The 'B' person must start the dialogue by saying 'You promised...' The children continue their improvisations from there.

When all of the children understand what is expected, ask them to start their improvised conversations. Allow these dialogues to run for up to two minutes.

Now ask the children to **swap roles**, so that the 'A' person leads the conversation with the same line. Again, allow the improvisations to continue for up to two minutes.

When all of the children have enacted both roles, thank them all for their efforts. Ask them to sit in a circle with you, and end with...

CIRCLE

CHILDREN REFLECT ON AND EVALUATE THEIR SKILLS AND KNOWLEDGE

Ask the children whether they enjoyed the drama session. Invite opinions and reasons.

- What do they think they have learned from and achieved in the session?
- What do they feel they have done well? What could they have done better?
- How do they think these activities could help them when they are performing?
- What do they now know about the story of *The Pied Piper of Hamelin*?

This information could be used as a basis for future workshop sessions.

SESSION 4

CHARACTERIZATION AND ROLE-PLAY

Timing: Spend up to 20 minutes on each activity. The whole session should take no more than 60 minutes.

Resources: A large space (such as the school hall); chairs; a toy telephone (optional).

Objectives: To explore the characters in the play. To encourage the appropriate use of movement and language in role-play.

CHARACTER REACTIONS

INTRODUCES CHARACTERIZATION

Sit the children together. Place a chair in a space close by, where they can all see it.

Ask the children to think about the different **characters** in *The Pied Piper of Hamelin*. They need to consider how these different characters could be portrayed through vocal expression, facial expression and body language.

Explain that you will ask for volunteers to step forward, **in role** as a particular character from the play, and **react to** the chair. They should approach the chair and sit on it, or react to it in some other way, in the style and manner of their chosen character.

Request or nominate volunteers in turn to react to the chair **in character**. Ask each child to specify which character he or she has chosen prior to starting the role-play. Each volunteer should play a different character (different rats, children and so on are acceptable). Praise each performance in turn.

When several children have reacted in character to the chair, thank all the children for their efforts and move on to...

ANSWER THAT PHONE!

DEVELOPS THE USE OF LANGUAGE IN ROLE

Sit the children in a circle. Place a chair in the centre of the circle, perhaps with a toy telephone next to it. Explain that you are going to ask them to **improvise** telephone calls made by characters from the play. Invite suggestions regarding what kind of telephone calls the characters might make. Acknowledge all responses.

Give each child in the circle a number in sequence. Say that when you call out a child's number, he or she must sit on the chair in the centre, make a telephone call and act out one side of a conversation as a character from the play. The choice of character is up to the children, but their improvised telephone conversation must make it possible for others to recognize which role they are acting out.

Now say that when you call out a different number, the first child must leave the chair and the next participant must then sit on it and continue the same conversation, remaining in the original role selected. (If you are not using a prop telephone, the children should mime holding a telephone receiver.) Continue the activity until two or three children have improvised a telephone conversation in this manner.

Now say that when you call a number, the next person in the centre of the circle should start a new telephone call in the role of a different character from the play. Repeat the activity in this manner until various different numbers have been called, and children have improvised telephone conversations in role as a variety of characters from the play.

Thank the children for their efforts. Remove the chair and telephone (if any) from the centre of the circle, and move on to...

INSTANT IMPROVISATIONS

CONSOLIDATES ROLE-PLAYING SKILLS AND IMPROVES CONCENTRATION

Ask the children to find a partner and a space to work in. Ask them to note carefully the **space** they are standing in and **who** they are with.

Now ask them to **improvise** a discussion between two TOWNSPEOPLE complaining about the MAYOR. Allow these spontaneous improvisations to continue for a maximum of 20 seconds. Tell the children that they must remember this combination of **partner, place and improvisation** as 'Number 1'.

Ask the children to find a new partner and a new space to work in. Now ask them to perform a **mime** of two RATS enjoying their life in Hamelin. (Remind them that mime is action without any words or other sounds.) Allow this spontaneous mime to continue for a maximum of 20 seconds. Tell the children that they must remember this combination of partner, place and improvisation as 'Number 2'.

Ask the children to find a new partner and a new space to work in, and then to improvise 'Number 3': two CHILDREN playing together. Again, limit this to a maximum of 20 seconds. Repeat for 'Number 4': the MAYOR discussing with one of the CORPORATION possible ways of getting rid of the rats.

Now say that when you call out a number from 1 to 4, the children must go to the correct place with the right partner and perform the appropriate improvisation. Each improvisation must be continued from the point at which it ended the last time they did it.

Call the numbers randomly. Allow each improvisation to continue for a maximum of 30 seconds before calling the new number. The result will be lots of children dashing around, changing partners and places and enacting different improvisations – some with speech, some without!

Repeat until each number between 1 and 4 has been called at least twice. Then stop the exercise and thank the children for their efforts. Call them back into a circle and end with...

CIRCLE

CHILDREN REFLECT ON AND EVALUATE THEIR SKILLS AND KNOWLEDGE

Ask the children whether they enjoyed the drama session. Invite opinions and reasons.

- What do they think they have learned from and achieved in it?
- What do they feel they have done well? What could they have done better?
- How do they think these activities could help them when they are performing?
- What have they learnt about the characters in *The Pied Piper of Hamelin*?

This information could be used as a basis for future workshop sessions.

SESSION 5
CONSOLIDATING PERFORMANCE SKILLS

Timing: Spend up to 20 minutes on each activity. The whole session should take no more than 60 minutes.

Resources: A large space (such as the school hall); the A3 story outline from Session 2; one copy per child of the playscript, and one for the teacher; chairs (optional); an A3 sheet of paper and pen (optional).

Objectives: To consolidate knowledge of the play. To concentrate performance skills.

CHARACTER SITUATIONS
STIMULATES CREATIVE PERFORMANCE

Ask the children to form pairs or threes. Ask them to recall the different characters in *The Pied Piper of Hamelin*. Explain that you are going to give them a **setting** or **situation**, and that you want them to **improvise** how different characters would behave in those situations. Tell them that they should distribute the roles for their improvisations fairly. Say that planning and preparation time will be minimal, and no time will be allocated for rehearsal.

Some possible character situations are as follows (you may prefer to choose alternatives):

- CHILDREN buying sweets in a shop
- a TOWNSPERSON in a supermarket
- the MAYOR buying a pair of shoes
- members of the CORPORATION in a restaurant
- the PIED PIPER buying a new outfit
- RATS on a beach holiday.

Allow each improvisation to continue for no longer than one minute. The aim is to explore the behaviour of the characters in the play and to transfer that behaviour to settings outside the play. The children could change partners after each improvisation, or they could swap roles with their current partners.

Move around the room while the children are enacting their situations. Praise any expressive or realistic performances. When they have enacted a number of different situations, thank them and comment positively on their efforts. Move on to...

STORYLINE IMPROVISATION

CONSOLIDATES KNOWLEDGE OF THE TEXT AND DEVELOPS PERFORMANCE SKILLS

Put the children into groups of five to eight. Say that you want them to work in their groups to **perform** different sections of *The Pied Piper of Hamelin*.

Explain that they will use **actions** and **dialogue** (conversation and/or narration) to bring their section of the story to life **in their own words**. These improvisations of the different sections will then be acted out in sequence to make up a performance of the whole play.

Using the story outline sheet from Session 2, allocate each group up to three of the sequential sentences. Make sure that all the children are clear about which sentences have been allocated to their group and what they have to do.

Allow the children up to five minutes to plan and rehearse their storyline improvisations. Now ask the groups to show their performances in sequence to the class. Tell the children acting as the audience to remain silent while others are performing, and invite them to applaud after each group's improvisations.

Thank all the children for their work, and praise their efforts. Move quickly on to...

SCRIPT EXTRACTS

REINTRODUCES THE SCRIPT AND PREPARES THE CHILDREN FOR PERFORMANCE

Tell the children that you are going to ask them to **perform** sections of the script in groups. Their performances can either be simple readings or include

actions as well. Distribute copies of the script, retaining one for yourself.

Put the children into groups (ideally of mixed reading ability), and allocate script extracts for performance. Tell the children that some of them may have to speak the lines for more than one character. You could use the following extracts, or others of your choice:

- eight to twelve children – Scene 1
- eight to twelve children – Scenes 3 and 4
- eight to twelve children – Scene 5.

The performances can be static or moved; but the children should be encouraged to use vocal and facial expression. Allow the children up to eight minutes to read and rehearse their script extracts. Move from group to group, making sure that the parts have been distributed fairly and that all the children are working productively.

When the rehearsal time has elapsed, ask the groups to perform their script extracts in sequence. Insist on silence from the 'audience' while others are performing, and invite observers to applaud the actors after each performance.

When all of the groups have performed their extracts, thank the children and praise their efforts. Ask them to sit in a circle again. End with...

CIRCLE

CHILDREN REFLECT ON AND EVALUATE THEIR SKILLS AND KNOWLEDGE

Ask the children whether they enjoyed the drama session. Invite opinions and reasons. Ask them which aspects they enjoyed the most and the least. Can they give reasons why?

- What do they think they have learned or achieved from the session?
- What do they feel is the most important skill they have learned?
- What do they feel they have done well? What could they have done better?
- How do they feel about their performances?
- What would they change if they had the chance to perform again?
- What do they think is the most important thing to remember when performing to an audience?

Acknowledge all responses. Thank the children for their hard work, and praise their efforts. You may wish to record their answers on an A3 sheet of paper to provide a visual prompt during rehearsals of the play.

PERFORMANCE PLAYS

The Pied Piper of Hamelin

CAST LIST

Narrator 1	**Pied Piper**
Narrator 2	**Rat 1**
Narrator 3	**Rat 2**
Narrator 4	**Rat 3**
Narrator 5	**Rat 4**
Narrator 6	**Rat 5**
(The number of narrators	**Rat 6**
can be reduced or increased	**Rat 7**
as required.)	**Rat 8**
Townsperson 1	**Child 1**
Townsperson 2	**Child 2**
Townsperson 3	**Child 3**
Townsperson 4	**Child 4**
Mayor	**Child 5**
Corporation 1	**Child 6**
Corporation 2	*(the lame boy)*
Corporation 3	
Corporation 4	

There are 30 characters, plus possible additional narrators and/or non-speaking roles: rats, townspeople and/or children. Encourage any non-speakers to perform in unison with the others, using body language and facial expression.

SCENES

1. A street in Hamelin Town / the Town Hall.
2. The rats' hideout.
3. Streets in Hamelin Town / the River Weser.
4. The marketplace in Hamelin Town.
5. A street in Hamelin Town/ Koppelberg Hill.
6. Pied Piper's Street in Hamelin Town.

(Scenes 1 to 5 take place on July 22nd, 1376. Scene 6 takes place some years later.)

Photocopiable

NARRATORS: Tell the audience what's happening in the story. Link scenes. Start and end the play.

TOWNSPERSON 1: Upset about the situation, but can't think of a solution.

TOWNSPERSON 2: Very angry with the council. Leads the others to complain.

TOWNSPERSON 3: Also angry with the council and demands that they provide answers!

TOWNSPERSON 4: Quite nervous and moans a lot, but very supportive of the other townspeople.

MAYOR: Fat, lazy and very selfish. Breaks his promises.

CORPORATION 1: Fat, self-important and bossy. Enjoys being on the council.

CORPORATION 2: Always asking questions. Self-important, but slightly more honest than the others.

CORPORATION 3: Fat, selfish and concerned about losing the votes of the people of Hamelin.

CORPORATION 4: Self-centred, quite miserable and a worrier. Hates having to deal with problems.

PIED PIPER: A strange, enigmatic, magical man who is honest and trustworthy.

RAT 1: Unpleasant. Likes frightening people and biting babies.

RAT 2: Likes wandering around Hamelin, especially into cellars. Enjoys being alone.

RAT 3: Brave, with a large appetite – especially for soup!

RAT 4: Nasty little rat who really enjoys making people scream.

RAT 5: Intelligent, loves the comfortable life in Hamelin. Knows what the council are up to!

RAT 6: Always hungry and always eating – will eat anything!

RAT 7: Likes causing trouble, especially if it provides entertainment for the other rats.

RAT 8: A smart, clever rat with a strong sense of humour and fun.

CHILD 1: A kind child who worries about others.

CHILD 2: Always curious and asking questions.

CHILD 3: Slightly nervous and easily led by others.

CHILD 4: Always ready for fun and enjoyment.

CHILD 5: A leader. Always organizing others.

CHILD 6: Has difficulty walking, but always tries to join in.

Photocopiable

SCENE 1: A street in Hamelin Town / the Town Hall

NARRATORS 1 and 2 enter.

NARRATOR 1: Hamelin Town's in Brunswick, by famous Hanover city. The river Weser, deep and wide, washes its wall on the southern side. A pleasanter spot you never spied; but, when begins my ditty almost five hundred years ago, to see the townsfolk suffer so from vermin, was a pity.

RATS 1–8 enter and mime appropriate actions throughout the following.

NARRATOR 2: Rats! They fought the dogs and killed the cats, and bit the babies in the cradles, and ate the cheeses out of the vats, and licked the soup from the cooks' own ladles, split open the kegs of salted sprats, made nests inside men's Sunday hats, and even spoiled the women's chats by drowning their speaking with shrieking and squeaking in fifty different sharps and flats. At last the people in a body to the Town Hall came flocking.

NARRATORS 1 and 2 exit.
MAYOR and CORPORATION 1, 2, 3 & 4 enter with table and chairs, positioning them on one side of the stage. They all sit at the table.

MAYOR: We are facing a serious crisis concerning these vermin, gentlemen, and we must act quickly to resolve the situation.

CORPORATION 2: But what do we do? We've tried almost everything possible to drive them out, and we still haven't got rid of them.

MAYOR: *(Sighing)* I know.

CORPORATION 3: The problem seems to be getting even worse. They're killing our pets, biting babies and even eating the food! Two vats of cheese had to be thrown away last week because the rats had ruined it.

MAYOR: *(Sighing)* I know, I know.

CORPORATION 1: The townspeople of Hamelin are terrified. Some of them won't even step out of their houses now.

CORPORATION 3: And we must make sure that we keep the support of the people of Hamelin.

CORPORATION 4: We have to remember that these are the people who elected us, and they can get rid of us just as easily.

CORPORATION 1: We are all in danger of losing our jobs over this.

MAYOR: *(Sighing)* I know, I know, I know.

CORPORATION 4: And, if we don't do something soon, these rats will find their way into the Town Hall, and that would be a disaster of the highest proportions.

CORPORATION 2: *(To the MAYOR)* So what do you suggest we try next, Mayor?

MAYOR: *(Sighing)* I don't know. *(Pause)* I was rather hoping one of you would come up with an idea.

There is a long pause while they ALL try to think of something.

CORPORATION 2: Well I can't think of anything.

CORPORATION 3: Nor can I. My mind's a complete blank.

CORPORATION 4: I've thought and thought, but nothing new occurs to me either.

CORPORATION 1: *(To the MAYOR)* You're the leader of this town. I would respectfully suggest that the responsibility for our actions lies with you.

MAYOR: *(Getting angry)* But I don't know what to do! We've completely exhausted our list of possible solutions!

CORPORATION 4: *(Nods in agreement)* We tried bringing in cats to chase them away. The rats killed them.

Photocopiable

CORPORATION 2: *(Nods in agreement)* We tried poison, but it was the one thing they didn't eat!

CORPORATION 1: *(Nods in agreement)* We tried traps, but they didn't go anywhere near them.

CORPORATION 3: It's all been a complete waste of time! There are more rats now than when the problem first started! The people are becoming distressed and VERY angry.

ALL CORPORATION: *(In unsion, turning to look at the MAYOR)* What should we do, Mayor?

There is a long pause.

MAYOR: Well... *(Pause)* ...let's do nothing! It's a solution we haven't tried yet, isn't it? Maybe all the rats will just disappear on their own.

Everyone pauses to consider this.

CORPORATION 2: *(Nods in agreement)* I think that's a very good idea.

CORPORATION 4: *(Nods in agreement)* Excellent thinking. A completely fresh approach.

CORPORATION 3: *(Nods in agreement)* A wise move. At least the plan can't fail this time.

CORPORATION 1: *(Nods in agreement)* It certainly has a lot of potential.

MAYOR: Good! It appears then that we are all in agreement, gentlemen. Thank you.

The MAYOR and CORPORATION freeze in position.
ALL TOWNSPEOPLE enter on the opposite side of the stage.

TOWNSPERSON 4: I don't think I can cope with this situation for much longer! The rats are everywhere!

TOWNSPERSON 1: I know. I'm afraid to step out of my door now.

TOWNSPERSON 3: It doesn't matter whether we're inside or out now, does it? Not now that they've found their way into the buildings.

TOWNSPERSON 2: They seem to be making nests all over the place.

TOWNSPERSON 4: It's terrible! Life is just unbearable!

TOWNSPERSON 2: *(To the others)* I wonder what the Mayor and his wonderful Corporation will try next to get rid of them.

TOWNSPERSON 1: I don't know what they CAN do.

TOWNSPERSON 3: Well, it can't be any worse than everything else they've tried.

TOWNSPERSON 4: The only thing that could be worse would be if they decided to do nothing at all!

TOWNSPERSON 1: I wouldn't put that past them either.

TOWNSPERSON 2: No, it's exactly the sort of stupid decision they WOULD make!

TOWNSPERSON 1: I can't understand how we ended up with such a bunch of idiots in charge!

TOWNSPERSON 3: Well, I don't remember voting for them!

TOWNSPERSON 4: Nor do I! In fact, I don't think I've met anyone who DID vote for them.

TOWNSPERSON 2: Well, you probably have, but they don't want to admit it now.

TOWNSPERSON 1: And I can't say I blame them either.

TOWNSPERSON 2: *(Getting angry)* We should go to the Town Hall and insist that they tell us what they intend to do next.

Photocopiable

TOWNSPERSON 3: (*Also angry*) Yes! Let's pay our esteemed leaders a visit. I'm completely fed up with their endless meetings. What we need is action – and now!

NARRATOR 2 enters.
The MAYOR and CORPORATION unfreeze.
The TOWNSPEOPLE turn to face the MAYOR and CORPORATION, as if confronting them.
The MAYOR and CORPORATION stand, facing the TOWNSPEOPLE.

TOWNSPERSON 2: 'Tis clear...

NARRATOR 2: Cried they...

TOWNSPERSON 2: ...our Mayor's a noddy. And as for our Corporation – shocking!

TOWNSPERSON 1: (*Angrily*) To think we buy gowns lined with ermine for dolts that can't or won't determine what's best to rid us of our vermin!

TOWNSPERSON 4: (*Angrily, to the MAYOR and CORPORATION*) You hope, because you're old and obese, to find in the furry civic robe ease?

TOWNSPERSON 3: (*Angrily*) Rouse up, sirs! Give your brains a racking to find the remedy we're lacking, or, sure as fate,

ALL TOWNSPEOPLE: (*In unison, to the MAYOR and CORPORATION*) We'll send you packing!

TOWNSPEOPLE all exit. They are extremely angry.
The MAYOR and CORPORATION react in fear, exchanging worried glances.
Then they ALL sit down again.
NARRATORS 3 and 4 enter.

NARRATOR 2: At this, the Mayor and Corporation quaked with a mighty consternation. For an hour they sat in council. At length the Mayor broke silence:

Photocopiable

MAYOR: *(Unhappily)* For a guilder I'd my ermine gown sell. I wish I were a mile hence! It's easy to bid one rack one's brain – I'm sure my poor head aches again: I've scratched it so, and all in vain. Oh for a trap, a trap, a trap!

NARRATOR 2 exits.

NARRATOR 3: Just as he said this, what should hap at the chamber door but a gentle tap?

A knocking sound is heard offstage.
The MAYOR and CORPORATION all jump in fright.

MAYOR: Bless us!

NARRATOR 3: Cried the Mayor.

MAYOR: What's that?

NARRATOR 3: With the Corporation as he sat, looking little though wondrous fat; nor brighter was his eye, nor moister than a too-long-opened oyster, save when at noon his paunch grew mutinous for a plate of turtle, green and glutinous.

MAYOR: Only a scraping of shoes on the mat? Anything like the sound of a rat makes my heart go pit-a-pat! *(Pauses briefly)* Come in!

NARRATOR 4: The Mayor cried, looking bigger. And in did come the strangest figure!

The PIED PIPER enters.
The MAYOR and CORPORATION all react with astonishment.

NARRATOR 4: His queer long coat, from heel to head, was half of yellow and half of red, and he himself was tall and thin with sharp blue eyes, each like a pin, and light loose hair, yet swarthy skin, no tuft on cheek nor beard on chin, but lips where smiles went out and in. There was no guessing his kith and kin; and nobody could enough admire the tall man and his quaint attire. Quoth one:

Photocopiable

CORPORATION 3: It's as my great-grandsire, starting up at the Trump of Doom's tone, had walked this way from his painted tombstone!

The PIED PIPER moves towards the MAYOR and CORPORATION.

NARRATOR 4: He advanced to the council table, and...

PIED PIPER: Please your honours...

NARRATOR 4: ...said he...

PIED PIPER: I'm able, by means of a secret charm, to draw all creatures living beneath the sun, that creep or swim or fly or run, after me so as you never saw! And I chiefly use my charm on creatures that do people harm, the mole and toad and newt and viper; and people call me the Pied Piper.

NARRATOR 4: And here they noticed round his neck a scarf of red and yellow stripe, to match with his coat of the self-same check; and at the scarf's end hung a pipe; and his fingers, they noticed, were ever straying as if impatient to be playing upon this pipe, as low it dangled over his vesture so old-fangled.

PIED PIPER: Yet...

NARRATOR 4: ...said he...

PIED PIPER: ...poor piper as I am, in Tartary I freed the Cham, last June, from his huge swarms of gnats; eased in Asia the Nizam of a monstrous brood of vampire-bats; and as for what your brain bewilders – if I can rid your town of rats, will you give me a thousand guilders?

MAYOR AND CORPORATION: *(Look at each other briefly, then in unison)* One? Fifty thousand!

NARRATOR 3: Was the exclamation of the astonished Mayor and Corporation.

Photocopiable

NARRATORS 3 and 4 exit.
The PIED PIPER nods in acceptance of their offer and exits.

MAYOR: What a strange fellow!

CORPORATION 3: As I said, it was just as if my great-grandfather had risen from the dead.

CORPORATION 1: He certainly seemed to have a strange way about him.

CORPORATION 4: Still, if he can rid us of these rats, I don't care how spooky he is!

CORPORATION 2: I know we all agreed to it, but can we actually afford a thousand guilders?

MAYOR: Oh, it won't come to that, I'm sure. I mean, nothing has been written down on paper, has it? We'll deal with that little problem when – and if – he deals with the rats.

CORPORATION 3: If he rids Hamelin of these awful vermin, I'd happily give him every guilder I have.

CORPORATION 1: Definitely! That's one verbal contract I'd be pleased to honour.

MAYOR: Well, let's just wait and see what happens, shall we?

The MAYOR and CORPORATION exit, taking their furniture offstage with them.

SCENE 2: The rats' hideout

ALL RATS enter in turn. They mime various appropriate 'ratlike' actions and scurry constantly around the stage.

RAT 1: This is the life, isn't it? Endless food...

RAT 2: ...No one giving you any problems...

RAT 3: ...Left alone to enjoy ourselves...

RAT 4: ...Making women scream and scaring everyone half to death!

RAT 5: Can you believe the silly things they've tried to get rid of us?

RAT 6: I know – cats, for heaven's sake! They've never frightened me!

RAT 7: And that poison! Even my youngest knew all about that!

RAT 8: I know, it's quite pathetic really. This council just don't have a clue, do they?

RAT 3: Well, thank goodness they don't is what I say. Just leave me in peace to eat what I like.

RAT 2: And go where I want. There's nothing I like better than to scurry about in the cellars of houses.

RAT 1: I really enjoy rushing through the streets, making everyone jump out of the way!

RAT 4: _(In agreement)_ I know, it's excellent, isn't it? All that screaming and shrieking!

RAT 5: And all that lovely, lovely food, just waiting for us!

RAT 6: I've eaten so much in the last three days, I keep thinking I'll burst!

RAT 1: Aaah, this is the life!

RAT 2: Hamelin is just such a great place to live, isn't it?

RAT 5: *(Nods in agreement)* I don't think they'll ever be able to get rid of me.

RAT 7: All that lovely cheese!

RAT 3: All that delicious soup!

RAT 6: Huge kegs of sprats to eat!

RAT 1: Chubby little babies' fingers to bite!

RAT 4: Lots of comfortable places to sleep.

RAT 8: We've got the whole town to ourselves.

ALL RATS: *(In unison)* Lovely!

They ALL pause, but continue moving about.

RAT 5: It's just a bit irritating that they keep trying to get rid of us, though.

RAT 8: I know. I'm beginning to get very bored with that.

RAT 2: Still, you can't have everything, can you?

RAT 4: No – and we do have a wonderful time here, after all.

RAT 7: *(To the others)* Do you know where I feel like going now? *(The other RATS shake their heads.)* To the Town Hall, that's where! Don't you think that would be great fun?

The RATS all snigger nastily.

Photocopiable

RAT 8: Oh yes! Can't you just see that chubby little Mayor running round the table, trying to get away from us?

RAT 7: Shall we go? I know a way in.

RAT 3: Brilliant idea!

RAT 1: *(To all the RATS)* Come on! Last one there's a pathetic little mouse!

The RATS all exit quickly.

SCENE 3: Streets in Hamelin Town / the River Weser

NARRATORS 5 and 6 enter.
The PIED PIPER enters.

NARRATOR 5: Into the street the Piper stepped, smiling first a little smile, as if he knew what magic slept in his quiet pipe the while. Then, like a musical adept, to blow the pipe his lips he wrinkled; and green and blue his sharp eyes twinkled, like a candle-flame where salt is sprinkled. And ere three shrill notes the pipe uttered, you heard as if an army muttered; and the muttering grew to a grumbling; and the grumbling grew to a mighty rumbling; and out of the houses the rats came tumbling.

All RATS enter from various places. They are all curious about the sound and need to follow it.

RAT 3: What's that beautiful sound? It makes me think of lovely food.

RAT 6: Me too. I can almost taste it.

RAT 4: It feels like I'm being led towards the greatest feast of my life!

RAT 2: I'm thinking of all the things I like best. Smoked sausage... Edam cheese... sewers in midsummer...

Photocopiable

RAT 5:   I don't think I've ever heard anything so lovely. I've got to follow that sound!

The RATS continue moving and line up behind the PIED PIPER during the following speech.

NARRATOR 6:   Great rats, small rats, lean rats, brawny rats, brown rats, black rats, grey rats, tawny rats, grave old plodders, gay young friskers, fathers, mothers, uncles, cousins, cocking tails and pricking whiskers, families by tens and dozens, brothers, sisters, husbands, wives – followed the Piper for their lives.

NARRATORS 2 and 3 enter.
NARRATORS 5 and 6 exit.
The RATS are led by the PIED PIPER during the following speech and exit from the auditorium to indicate their 'drowning'.

NARRATOR 3:   From street to street he piped advancing, and step for step they followed dancing, until they came to the river Weser, wherein all plunged and perished! Save one who, strong as Julius Caesar, swam across and lived to carry (as he, the manuscript he cherished) to Ratland home his commentary, which was...

RAT 8 re-enters.

RAT 8:   At the first shrill notes of the pipe, I heard a sound as of scraping tripe; and putting apples, wondrous ripe, into a cider-press's gripe; and a moving away of pickle-tub boards, and a leaving ajar of conserve-cupboards, and a drawing of corks from train-oil flasks, and a breaking of hoops on butter-casks; and it seemed as if a voice (sweeter far than by harp or by psaltery Is breathed) called out, 'Oh rats, rejoice! The world is grown to one vast dry-saltery! So munch on, crunch on, take your nuncheon, breakfast, supper, dinner, luncheon!' And just as a bulky sugar-puncheon, all ready staved, like a great sun, shone glorious scarce an inch before me, just as methought it said, 'Come, bore me!' – I found the Weser rolling o'er me.

Photocopiable

NARRATOR 2: You should have heard the Hamelin people ringing the bells till they rocked the steeple.

SCENE 4: The marketplace in Hamelin Town

ALL TOWNSPEOPLE and ALL CHILDREN enter.

CHILD 1: The rats have all gone!

TOWNSPERSON 2: I know, isn't it wonderful?

CHILD 2: Where are they? Where have they disappeared to?

TOWNSPERSON 3: I don't know, but they've certainly all gone.

TOWNSPERSON 4: I heard that they'd all fallen into the river Weser and drowned.

TOWNSPERSON 1: Yes, I heard that as well. I wonder why?

TOWNSPERSON 2: Maybe the council found something to drive them away with.

TOWNSPERSON 3: Well, it took them long enough to do it!

TOWNSPERSON 4: People are saying that a strange man lured them all away.

TOWNSPERSON 2: Are they? Who was it?

TOWNSPERSON 4: I don't know. Someone the Mayor found, I think.

TOWNSPERSON 1: Well, whoever it was, I'd like to shake his hand.

CHILD 3: Does that mean they're not coming back, ever?

CHILD 4: Does that mean we can play in the streets again without worrying about being bitten and chased?

Photocopiable

TOWNSPERSON 2: It means that at last, we can all start living properly again.

CHILD 5: *(To other children)* Well, what are we waiting for? Let's go and play! Last one there's a sissy!

The CHILDREN all exit excitedly.
CHILD 6 struggles to follow them.

CHILD 6: Don't go so fast! I want to play too! Wait for me!

He exits slowly after the other CHILDREN.

TOWNSPERSON 3: It seems we may have underestimated our Mayor and his council.

TOWNSPERSON 4: Yes. *(Pause)* Exactly who did it and how they did it, I'm still not sure, but the rats have definitely all gone.

TOWNSPERSON 2: Well, I for one will certainly be voting for the Mayor again next year. It will be wonderful be able to to live a normal life again.

TOWNSPERSON 1: I think this occasion should be celebrated properly. I vote for an enormous party!

OTHER TOWNSPEOPLE: *(Ad libbing in agreement)* 'Yes!' 'What a great idea!' 'Good thought!' and so on.

NARRATOR 2 enters.
The MAYOR and ALL CORPORATION enter on the opposite side of the stage.
The TOWNSPEOPLE applaud them.
The MAYOR and CORPORATION acknowledge the applause modestly. Some of them bow slightly.
The MAYOR addresses the TOWNSPEOPLE directly.

MAYOR: Go...

NARRATOR 2: ...cried the Mayor...

Photocopiable

MAYOR: ...and get long poles, poke out the nests and block up the holes! Consult with carpenters and builders, and leave in our town not a trace of the rats!

NARRATOR 1 enters.
The PIED PIPER enters.

NARRATOR 2: When suddenly, up the face of the Piper perked in the marketplace, saying...

PIED PIPER: First, if you please, my thousand guilders!

The MAYOR signals to the TOWNSPEOPLE that they should leave. The TOWNSPEOPLE all exit, slightly puzzled about who the Pied Piper is and what's happening. The MAYOR and the CORPORATION look nervous, but determined. They exchange glances.

NARRATOR 2: A thousand guilders! The Mayor looked blue; so did the Corporation too. For council dinners made rare havoc with Claret, Moselle, Vin-de-Grave, Hock; and half the money would replenish their cellar's biggest butt with Rhenish. To pay this sum to a wandering fellow with a gipsy coat of red and yellow!

The MAYOR gathers all the CORPORATION for a meeting while the PIED PIPER looks on.

MAYOR: *(To the others)* I don't think we can afford a thousand guilders, can we?

CORPORATION 1: *(Unsure)* Well, we can if we reduce our wine cellar and cut down on our drinking.

CORPORATION 2: And don't have so many council dinners.

CORPORATION 3: And stop being driven around in limousines.

CORPORATION 4: And, maybe, sell off a few of our robes and chains.

MAYOR: So we can't afford it, then?

Photocopiable

Pause. They all look at each other.

ALL CORPORATION: (*In unison*): No, we can't.

MAYOR: Right! (*He pauses, thinking carefully, and then beckons the PIED PIPER over.*) Beside...

NARRATOR 2: ...quoth the Mayor with a knowing wink,

MAYOR: Our business was done at the river's brink. We saw with our eyes the vermin sink, and what's dead can't come to life I think. So, friend, we're not the folks to shrink from the duty of giving you something for drink, and a matter of money to put in your poke; but as for the guilders, what we spoke of them, as you very well know, was in joke. Besides, our losses have made us thrifty. A thousand guilders? Come, take fifty!

The MAYOR offers the PIED PIPER a small bag of money.

NARRATOR 1: The Piper's face fell and he cried...

PIED PIPER: (*Furious*) No trifling! I can't wait, beside! I've promised to visit by dinnertime Baghdad – and accept the prime of the Head Cook's potage, all he's rich in, for having left, in the Caliph's kitchen, of a nest of scorpions no survivor. With him I proved no bargain-driver. With you, don't think I'll bate a stiver! And folks who put me in a passion may hear me pipe in another fashion.

The PIED PIPER throws the small bag of money down at the MAYOR'S feet in disgust.

MAYOR: (*Also furious*) How...?

NARRATOR 1: ...cried the Mayor...

MAYOR: ...d'ye think I brook being worse treated than a cook? Insulted by a lazy ribald with idle pipe and vesture piebald? You threaten us, fellow? Do your worst. Blow your pipe there till you burst!

Photocopiable

NARRATORS 1 and 2 exit.
The PIED PIPER exits, angrily.
The MAYOR picks up the small bag of money. There is a short, awkward pause.

CORPORATION 3: Well, I think you handled that slight embarrassment very well.

CORPORATION 4: Yes, he couldn't argue with that logic, could he?

CORPORATION 2: The cheek of the fellow, expecting to be paid when all he'd done was drown the rats!

CORPORATION 3: Well, they drowned themselves really, didn't they?

CORPORATION 4: Exactly! And the people of Hamelin are happy, which is all that matters.

CORPORATION 2: I see no point in disappointing them by telling them the truth.

CORPORATION 1: Well, we could have drowned them, anyway, if we'd thought of it first. *(To the MAYOR)* I think you were very generous in your offer.

MAYOR: *(Showing off)* Yes, I did deal with him remarkably well, didn't I? I suppose that's what comes of having years of experience in handling this sort of situation.

CORPORATION 2: What do you think he'll do? He seemed very angry.

MAYOR: Do? What can he do? He can hardly bring all the rats back again, can he?

The MAYOR looks around at all of the others for support and they all laugh, some slightly nervously.

MAYOR: Besides, it's not as if I've offered him nothing, is it? I made what I felt was a very fair proposal.

CORPORATION 1: It was very fair indeed – and I'm sure that, once he's had a chance to calm down, the gentleman will be happy to accept.

CORPORATION 3: *(To CORPORATION 2)* I don't think we need to worry too much about this. The rats have gone and our jobs are safe – that's all that matters.

CORPORATION 4: Exactly. I couldn't agree more. The crisis has been resolved, and life in Hamelin can go back to normal.

The MAYOR and all the CORPORATION continue to congratulate themselves as they exit.

SCENE 5: A street in Hamelin Town / Koppelberg Hill

NARRATORS 1 and 5 enter.
The PIED PIPER enters.

NARRATOR 1: Once more he stepped into the street, and to his lips again laid his long pipe of smooth straight cane; and ere he blew three notes (such sweet soft notes as yet musician's cunning never gave the enraptured air), there was a rustling that seemed like a bustling of merry crowds justling at pitching and hustling; small feet were pattering, wooden shoes clattering, little hands clapping and little tongues chattering; and, like fowls in a farmyard when barley is scattering, out came the children running.

NARRATOR 5: All the little boys and girls, with rosy cheeks and flaxen curls, and sparkling eyes and teeth like pearls, tripping and skipping, ran merrily after the wonderful music with shouting and laughter.

ALL CHILDREN enter, one at a time.

CHILD 2: What's that beautiful sound? It reminds me of somewhere wonderful.

CHILD 5: It's so lovely, I just have to follow it.

CHILD 3: I keep thinking of glorious fruit trees and brightly-coloured flowers. Where is it?

CHILD 1: Can you hear that music? Isn't it wonderful?

CHILD 4: That sound is going to take us somewhere really special!

CHILD 2: How can we get there?

CHILD 3: I have to go to this new country!

CHILD 5: I don't want to stay in Hamelin. I want to go to the beautiful place of the music!

CHILD 2: *(Indicating the PIED PIPER)* He's leading us there!

CHILD 4: Follow him to the wonderful new land!

They follow the PIED PIPER off the stage, into and through the auditorium, moving slowly and happily.
CHILD 6 enters just as they are following.

CHILD 6: Don't go so fast! I have to come too! I won't be lame in the beautiful place. Please wait for me!

CHILD 6 slowly follows the PIED PIPER and the rest of the CHILDREN into the auditorium.
The MAYOR and CORPORATION enter on stage.
NARRATORS 1 and 5 exit.
NARRATORS 4 and 6 enter.
The TOWNSPEOPLE enter on the opposite side of the stage.

TOWNSPERSON 2: *(Worried)* What's happening? Where are all the children going?

TOWNSPERSON 4: *(Shouting to the MAYOR)* Stop him, Mayor! Do something!

TOWNSPERSON 3:   *(Upset)* Why is he taking our children away? *(Shouting)* Come back, come back!

The TOWNSPEOPLE, MAYOR and CORPORATION all watch in horrified silence, gradually realising what is happening as NARRATOR 4 speaks.

NARRATOR 4:   The Mayor was dumb, and the council stood as if they were changed into blocks of wood, unable to move a step or cry to the children merrily skipping by – could only follow with the eye that joyous crowd at the Piper's back. But how the Mayor was on the rack, and the wretched council's bosoms beat, as the Piper turned from the High Street to where the Weser rolled its waters right in the way of their sons and daughters! However, he turned from south to west, and to Koppelberg Hill his steps addressed, and after him the children pressed; great was the joy in every breast.

The PIED PIPER leads the CHILDREN towards an exit in the auditorium. CHILD 6 struggles to keep up but fails.

TOWNSPERSON 1:   *(Panicking)* He never can cross that mighty top! He's forced to let the piping drop, and we shall see our children stop!

NARRATOR 6:   When, lo, as they reached the mountainside, a wondrous portal opened wide as if a cavern were suddenly hollowed; and the Piper advanced and the children followed. And when all were in to the very last, the door in the mountainside shut fast.

The PIED PIPER and CHILDREN exit through a door which closes firmly on them.
The doors close just as CHILD 6 reaches them, and he is denied entry.
The MAYOR, CORPORATION and TOWNSPEOPLE all react to what they have seen.
CHILD 6 returns sadly to the stage.

TOWNSPERSON 4:   What happened? Koppelberg Hill just opened up and swallowed our children!

TOWNSPERSON 3:   I don't believe what I just saw! Where did they go?

Photocopiable

TOWNSPERSON 2: They've disappeared! He's taken our children away from us.

NARRATOR 6: Did I say all? No! One was lame, and could not dance the whole of the way; and in after years, if you would blame his sadness, he was used to say –

CHILD 6: It's dull in our town since my playmates left! I can't forget that I'm bereft of all the pleasant sights they see, which the Piper also promised me. For he led us, he said, to a joyous land, joining the town and just at hand, where waters gushed and fruit trees grew, and flowers put forth a fairer hue, and everything was strange and new. The sparrows were brighter than peacocks here, and their dogs outran our fallow deer, and honey-bees had lost their stings, and horses were born with eagles' wings. And just as I became assured my lame foot would be speedily cured, the music stopped and I stood still, and found myself outside the hill, left alone against my will, to go now limping as before, and never hear of that country more.

CHILD 6 exits sadly.
NARRATORS 3 and 5 enter and stand silently in position.

TOWNSPERSON 1: *(To the MAYOR and CORPORATION, angrily)* What did you say to him? What did you do that made him take our children from us?

MAYOR: *(Nervous and upset)* We didn't do or say anything. *(To the CORPORATION)* Did we, gentlemen?

CORPORATION 2: I thought he'd be angry. *(To the MAYOR)* You should have paid him.

MAYOR: But we all agreed!

CORPORATION 4: *(To the MAYOR)* No, we didn't. YOU spoke to him. YOU handled it. It was all your idea!

CORPORATION 3: *(Agreeing)* We just followed your instructions.

Photocopiable

CORPORATION 1: *(Agreeing)* Exactly. It wasn't us who broke our promise!

MAYOR: *(To TOWNSPEOPLE)* Don't worry, I'll find him and fetch your children back. I won't rest until all of the children are safely home again in Hamelin.

TOWNSPERSON 2: *(Sadly)* Neither will we, Mayor. Neither will we.

The TOWNSPEOPLE exit sadly. The MAYOR and CORPORATION exit, continuing to argue with each other, with the CORPORATION verbally attacking the MAYOR. NARRATORS 3, 4, 5 and 6 remain on stage in their positions for Scene 6.

SCENE 6: Pied Piper's Street, Hamelin Town

Narrators 3, 4, 5 and 6 still in their positions.

NARRATOR 3: Alas, alas for Hamelin! There came into many a burgher's pate a text which says that heaven's gate opes to the rich at as easy a rate as the needle's eye takes a camel in! The Mayor sent east, west, north and south, to offer the Piper, by word of mouth wherever it was men's lot to find him, silver and gold to his heart's content, if he'd only return the way he went and bring the children behind him.

NARRATORS 1 and 2 enter.

NARRATOR 5: But when they saw 'twas a lost endeavour, and Piper and dancers were gone for ever, they made a decree that lawyers never should think their records dated duly if, after the day of the month and year, these words did not as well appear: 'And so long after what happened here on the twenty-second of July, thirteen hundred and seventy-six'. And the better in memory to fix the place of the children's last retreat, they called it the Pied Piper's Street –

(NARRATOR 2 puts up a sign which reads 'PIED PIPER'S STREET')

NARRATOR 5: Where anyone playing on pipe or tabor was sure for the future to lose his labour.

NARRATOR 2: Nor suffered they hostelry or tavern to shock with mirth a street so solemn; but opposite the place of the cavern they wrote the story on a column; and on the great church-window painted the same, to make the world acquainted with how the children were stolen away; and there it stands to this very day.

NARRATOR 4: And I must not omit to say that in Transylvania there's a tribe of alien people who ascribe the outlandish ways and dress on which their neighbours lay such stress to their fathers and mothers having risen out of some subterraneous prison into which they were trepanned a long time ago in a mighty band out of Hamelin town in Brunswick land; but how or why, they don't understand.

NARRATOR 1: *(Talking directly to NARRATOR 2)* So, Willy, let you and me be wipers of scores out with all men – especially pipers! And, whether they pipe us free from rats or from mice, if we've promised them aught, let us keep our promise!

ALL NARRATORS stand still in their positions.
The lights fade to blackout.
The curtains close.

END

AUDITIONS AND CASTING

The easiest way to start the audition process is to read through the play with the children two or three times. The initial reading should be used simply to familiarize the children with the material; allocate speeches, reading in sequence around the circle. In the second read-through, let the children volunteer to read specific character parts; in the third, nominate specific children to read certain character parts. During the second and third readings, encourage the children to think about using vocal expression, following the stage directions and picking up their cues quickly. Write yourself notes on how the children perform when reading specific roles. At any read-through, you must give every child a chance to read something.

Please make a concerted effort to allow less confident readers a chance to read, encouraging others in the group to show patience and consideration when listening. Plays always help poor readers to develop their language skills, and their enthusiasm for performance often leads to a great deal of work away from rehearsals to make sure that they know their lines. A poor reader does not necessarily make a poor actor.

There are several alternative methods of casting your play, some of which are described below. The process can be as formal or informal as you wish.

FORMAL AUDITIONS

These can be held by selecting specific speeches or scenes from the play and asking the children to learn and recite these, or read them through, in various group combinations. The disadvantages of this method are that it takes an inordinate amount of time to plan and execute, and that it makes children very tense and often unable to perform well – especially if their memory skills are not strong. (Even if they are reading the text, a successful audition will depend on their being very familiar with it.)

CHILDREN CHOOSING THEIR OWN ROLES

Another option is to ask the children to write their first and second role choices, confidentially, on pieces of paper. Ask them to try and make sure the spelling is correct, and also to put their full names on the slips of paper. Some children will only have one choice of role; some will go for the same first choice; and there will be some children who 'don't care' what role they are given. Gather all the pieces of paper together; in

a quiet place at another time, sit down and work out who wants what and which role combinations would work. Try to be as fair as possible, both to the children and to the play. Children are often aware of their 'failings' as actors, and usually accept that others have stronger performance skills; but this doesn't prevent many children from feeling acute disappointment if they fail to secure the role they are desperate for.

When allocating roles after using this method, sit the children in a circle and read from the bottom of the cast list upwards, giving the name of the character first and the name of the child who has been given that part after. Sometimes a little of what is known as 'director speak' (see page 40) may come in handy for convincing upset children that they are more suited to smaller 'character roles' than to a main part. After each part has been given out, allow the children up to five minutes to discuss the casting and to accept and compare their roles.

DRAWING NAMES OUT OF A HAT

Another method which is fairer, but more risky for your play, is to ask the children to put their names into a hat and then to draw a name for each character. Children have mixed feelings about this process: there is always a possibility that their name will be drawn for the character they want to play, but they know this is not very likely. Also, less confident children can sometimes end up with large roles which they don't feel happy or comfortable with performing.

CHOOSING ACTORS YOURSELF

The final option is simply to allocate the roles yourself, choosing children that you know are able and confident. However, this can upset other children who are rarely given the opportunity to perform, and removes any sense of the children being involved in the casting process.

After a number of years and arguments, floods of tears and several very unhappy children, I have reached the conclusion that the second method is the fairest and surest option. It gives children a chance to specify which roles they would like to perform, and gives you the opportunity to make a final decision in a considered manner. It always surprises me which parts children choose to go for, and which appear to be the most popular! Sometimes children who appear confident – and who might have otherwise been given a major role – can select small roles; likewise, children who appear less confident can select major roles.

I feel very strongly that children's enthusiasm for playing their roles will result in an easier rehearsal process, an eagerness to learn lines and a willingness to throw themselves into the role wholeheartedly. I have been vindicated in this belief over and over again when 'risking' a major part on a child who might not have been given a chance to shine had I used a different method of casting.

Whichever casting method you have used, you should now ask the children to sit in a circle and arrange them according to character or family groups. Read through the play again together, to get the feel of how it sounds with all the roles established.

Finally, tell the children that each person in the cast is as important as the next: without any one character, you don't have a full team and, therefore, a complete play. They won't believe you – they've already spent time counting the number of lines they have to say – but it **is** true, and needs to be expressed.

DIRECTOR SPEAK

Whatever decisions you make about casting, and however fair you try to be, there will be children who are upset when the parts are allocated. Many children feel that they never have the opportunity to show what they can do; some can build up quite a strong resentment against others who always seem to get the main roles; and quieter children can feel a sense of failure at not having pushed themselves forward yet again.

These feelings need to be dealt with as sensitively and as quickly as possible, away from the main group. In these situations you must employ what is known as 'director speak' in an attempt to pacify, boost and reassure the children. This means using a variety of statements aimed to placate, such as:

● *I know you're upset about not getting the part you wanted, but I really needed a good actor for that scene to encourage all the others to perform well.*
● *I understand that you wanted a main part, but you read this part so well that I just had to give it to you.*
● *I appreciate that you're disappointed; but I wanted to give you the chance to try something different this time, to show me what you could do.*
● *I know that you're unhappy, but can you understand that I have to be fair to everyone and give others a chance to try a bigger part sometimes?*

And others of a similar nature. The children will probably recognize that you are trying to pacify them; but what is important about using 'director speak' is

that you are hearing and acknowledging their feelings of unhappiness, and that they have had an opportunity to express these feelings.

Whatever you say isn't going to make a lot of difference to some children. In these cases, they need to be given a straightforward choice between playing the part they have been given and not being in the play at all – however cruel that may seem. Most children will choose the former option. Any child opting out of the play should be kept occupied with other tasks, such as painting scenery, prompting or making props and costumes. They will often regret their decision to pull out; if possible, they should be given the chance to join in again.

The main aspect of the production of a play which is likely to anger and upset children is the part allocation. So if, when using 'director speak' on a previous occasion, you have promised someone a bigger part next time, you must keep your promise! Also, if you have stated that 'everyone needs to be given a chance', then do not under any circumstances allocate the main roles to the same children as were chosen last time.

I use 'director speak' all the time, and try to use it in a way that is reasonable, fair and understanding. Used in that way, it works.

STRUCTURING REHEARSALS

When you're faced with directing a play, it's sometimes difficult to know what to tackle first. You have a large group of children awaiting your instructions, a limited amount of access to the school hall, and very little time! Good pre-rehearsal planning and preparation is therefore essential. The following timetable has always worked for me, and might be useful for you.

PREPARATION
Immediately after casting, spend an hour or two resolving practical issues: what sort of stage the play will be performed on; how many entrances and exits the stage will have, and where these will be (plus a consideration of what imaginary setting lies beyond them); where the children will go when they are not on stage; exactly how and where each character enters and exits; what scenery, furniture and props you will have (if any), and where these will be positioned on the stage; whether any characters will enter from other parts of the auditorium and if so, where they will enter from. All of these points need to be clearly defined to your own satisfaction **before you start rehearsals**.

REHEARSALS 1 TO 3

These should be used to complete what is known as 'blocking': simply specifying the movements of the children on, off and around the stage. Explain your staging ideas to the cast, marking out the stage area and exits using chairs. Tell them what furniture and scenery will be on stage, and use chairs or other equipment to represent this as well. Take time to make sure that all of the cast are familiar with the setting, the acting area and their movements before continuing. They'll be desperate to get on with the 'acting' – but it is essential that they understand the space they are working in, and know their own moves, before they try to go any further. It is impossible to teach children to act **and** give them instructions about where to enter and exit at the same time!

REHEARSALS 4 TO 8

Break the play down into small sections and rehearse these individually. **Don't** try to work through the whole play in a single rehearsal at this point. Start from the beginning and work through a **maximum** of three scenes. Rehearse the same section a number of times, until you feel that familiarity is beginning to reduce interest; then move on to the next section.

Continue the next rehearsal from where you left off the last time; never repeat the previous section and then move on, or the result will be one or two sections that are absolutely brilliant and a number that are completely under-rehearsed. (I speak from experience!) This will mean that some children are unoccupied for some of the rehearsals. Set them learning their lines in pairs, watching the play and making notes, giving you feedback about how it looks, making props, designing posters and programmes, and so on. Insist that they remain aware of what is going on – they could be called into rehearsal at any time!

Carry on rehearsing the play in small sections until you have completed the whole script.

Make notes as you go along of any potential difficulties; any scenes or characters which you feel will need extra rehearsing; and any ideas that you have for scenery, props, costumes or effects.

REHEARSALS 9 TO 11

Rehearse the complete play at each rehearsal. Use these rehearsals to concentrate on scenes or sections which need extra attention. Try to get through the whole play at least once during each rehearsal period, but don't panic if you fail to do so! Again, never go back over sections: always start the next rehearsal from the point at which you finished the last one. (Sections that have gone wrong should be repeated afterwards or at a later date, not straight away.)

REHEARSALS 12 TO 14

These should be used for complete run-throughs: a **technical rehearsal** to go over any lights, sound effects, props or music you might be including; and two **dress rehearsals** complete with costumes and make-up. Spend ten minutes at the beginning of the final dress rehearsal to work out and practise your 'curtain call', then run through the play completely without stopping. Final rehearsals are always a nightmare: the children are stressed and excited, you're stressed and beginning to panic, and everyone seems to be snapping at each other! Try to keep the children occupied at all times; plan what you want to achieve in the rehearsals, and try to stick to your plan.

I appreciate that this is a rehearsal structure for an 'ideal world', one which doesn't take into account those little things sent to try us: children being absent, falling out, not learning their lines or forgetting everything they learnt at the last rehearsal; props and costumes failing to materialize; and so on... But those stresses are what give us the sense of achievement when the play finally goes on – and it **does** always go on, despite the horrendous feeling that it will fail. The old saying 'It'll be all right on the night' always applies!

STAGING AND SCENERY

The Pied Piper of Hamelin can be very simple to stage. It was first performed on a 'proscenium arch' stage: a square, raised stage resembling a box, with structured spaces at the side for 'wings' and full curtains. (See picture on page 42.) There was no set at all: the stage was completely bare, and any furniture (used only by the MAYOR and CORPORATION) was brought on, positioned and removed by the actors playing those roles. The only drawback of performing on a bare stage is that the children need to work harder in their acting to establish settings and create atmosphere.

The majority of the characters simply walked on from the wings (the sides of the stage) to make their entrances, and exited in the same manner. However, the auditorium (where the audience sit) was widely used for additional entrances and exits. This provided variety and interest, and enabled the PIED PIPER to lead both rats and children away from the village in a long procession. The hall I used was blessed with three different auditorium exits; one was utilised as a general 'come and go' exit, and the other two represented the river Weser and Koppleberg Hill respectively.

A particularly dramatic effect was created using a double-doored exit at the back of the hall, with helpers opening and closing the doors on time as the Hamelin children were 'swallowed up' by the mountain and CHILD 6 was poignantly shut out.

The audience accepted the different settings in the play without any need for elaborate scenery. The play can work if performed simply against black curtains, using a variety of entrances and exits to represent different places in and around the village. However, if you want to be more adventurous and use scenery, several options are open to you.

If you are performing on a proscenium arch stage, the solid back wall (known as the **cyclorama**, or **cyc.**) can be decorated with fixed scenery that is appropriate for all the scenes in the play. This might consist of a general 'brick wall' pattern, painted house fronts, or trees and flowers. Alternatively, the 'general theme' idea can be taken a step further by decorating the proscenium arches themselves with a brickwork pattern, or with trees and flowers, and the cyc. with a backdrop of the outside of various village buildings. Scenery can be painted on large sheets of lining paper or fabric and fixed to the arches to avoid permanent painting. Similarly, paper scenery can be attached to the cyc. if it is unfeasible to decorate that permanently. Just make sure that whatever you use to attach the scenery holds it up well!

If you are performing on a raised rostrum (as in many schools), you could create simple wooden or cardboard screens to act as the wings (on either side of the stage) and the back wall, and decorate these with house fronts, general brickwork or trees and flowers. Room dividers work well for this. Again, these screens can remain in place throughout the play, and will act as a permanent backdrop for all of the scenes.

If, however, you wish to change the scenery for each

different setting, you will obviously need some changeable backdrops. If you have a pulley system in your school, you can use this to hang a painted backdrop. However, you are limited to the number of backdrops you can fit on a pulley system, and so this method is not ideal. Other options include:

● Painting scenery onto large sheets of fabric and draping these over a long clothes rail (the type you find in warehouses or large stores). The rail can be swung round on castors to show the other side of any painted cloth, providing an instant scene change!
● Painting scenery onto large wooden or cardboard screens with castors attached, and wheeling these on to provide a moveable backdrop.
● Asking any 'handy' carpenters to make a large wooden frame, approximately 8' × 6'. Attach a large piece of muslin or cotton fabric to it firmly, then stretch the fabric tightly across and around the edge of the frame. Fix castors to the bottom of the frame, and paint your scenery onto it. It can then be wheeled on to provide an instant backdrop. Fabric could be attached to both sides of the frame, providing two backdrops. The main problem then is getting the large screens on and off the stage, and storing them when they are not in use!
● Fixing a long, detachable pole across the back of the stage area and attaching several pieces of fabric, with a different scene painted on each one, in a 'flip chart' arrangement. The backdrops can then be 'flipped over' at appropriate points.
● Using the same detachable pole, but drawing the fabric like a curtain across the back of the staging area. This will only provide one scenery change, however.

Whatever you choose, please remember two important things:
1. There is no shame in choosing fixed scenery as an option. It's much better to spend what time and resources you have in creating a wonderful, elaborate setting that remains fixed than to fail in trying to create a large variety of different scenery effects.
2. If you choose to have movable scenery, remember that **someone** has to be responsible for bringing it on (at the right moment) and taking it off (at the right moment) – and that you have to find somewhere for it to 'live' when it is not in use!

ADDITIONAL STAGING NOTES
● Consider how you can create interesting effects by varying the entrances and exits that your actors use.
● Nominate specific entrances and stage positions for the narrators, and retain these throughout the play. Giving them fixed entrances and positions in this way not only makes it easier for the actors to remember

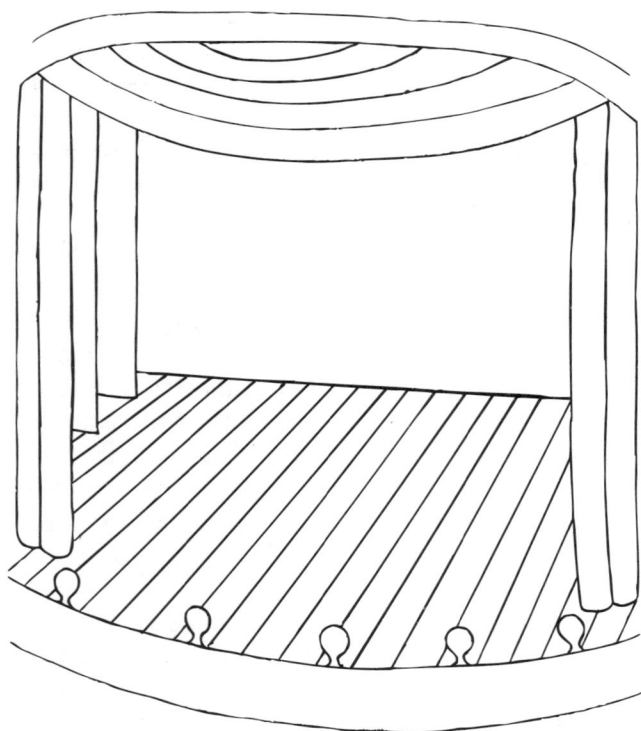

their stage directions, it also creates a nice sense of anticipation and consistency.

● Work hard on the timing of movements! I spent an awful lot of time working with the narrators, the rats and the children to make sure that their exits worked in harmony with the script. It's time-consuming, but well worth the effort.

LIGHTING

Lighting in a play is used to establish time, enhance setting and create atmosphere. If you are lucky enough to have a professional lighting rig, you can produce some wonderful lighting effects. If not, simple lighting is often sufficient to establish the basics. Our production of *The Pied Piper of Hamelin* was lit very simply with what is known as a 'general wash': the stage was completely lit up. The action of the play takes place over a single day, reducing the necessity for time changes and allowing the lighting to remain constant throughout.

If you have a dimmer switch, use this to good effect – especially for the rats' hideout in Scene 2. If you don't have the facility to dim lights, you can leave them on full for the whole play; alternatively, you can switch off one or two lights to give the impression of a dark and gloomy atmosphere.

If you have a professional lighting rig, you could use coloured 'gels' to create some atmospheric lighting. These are transparencies which fit over your spotlights, giving them a coloured glow. They must be purchased from a theatre lighting specialist, because they need to be heat-resistant. A couple of spotlights with blue gels attached, combined with a couple of clear white spotlights, will give an excellent gloomy effect for the rats' hideout.

In Scene 6, the mood becomes sombre; again, if you have the facility, the lights can be dimmed slightly to express this. A slow fade to blackout (extinguishing all lights) at the end of the play will result in some effective dramatic tension, and close the play in a powerful way.

For a stage with no front curtains, switching off or dimming lights can also be used to blackout the stage during scene changes, or in preparation for the 'curtain call' – but please make sure that your actors practise moving around in the dark!

MUSIC AND SOUND EFFECTS

Music can be used effectively to set the scene. Choose any songs which highlight the theme of broken promises, mention rats, or reflect the historical or geographical setting. Pick one as an opening piece of music, and repeat it at the end of the play. This will act as a 'curtain', telling the audience when the play has started and finished. You should check that your school has the relevant licences to broadcast music at a public event.

Other musical extracts can be included at various points during the play:

● After NARRATOR 2's first section of narration, music could be used to introduce the MAYOR and CORPORATION. Many numbers from *Gilbert and Sullivan* could be adapted for this.
● On the PIED PIPER's first entrance (after NARRATOR 4's line *And in did come the strangest figure!*), something with a theme of 'strangers' or 'magic' would be effective.
● Music with a fast tempo would be ideal to introduce the RATS in Scene 2. A 'dance' could be devised for those playing the RATS.
● The 'rat' music could be repeated softly as they are led by the PIED PIPER in Scene 3.
● An 'upbeat' choral number could be used to introduce Scene 4 – for example, 'On a Wonderful Day Like Today' or 'Zip A Dee Doo Dah'.
● A children's playground song or nursery song could be included during Scene 5, either after NARRATOR 1's speech or playing softly as they are led away by the PIED PIPER.
● Something slow and melancholy could underscore the narration in Scene 6 – or the theme for the children could be played again, more slowly or in a minor key.

With regard to the PIED PIPER playing music from his pipe – in my production, he didn't! I did consider trying to cue recorded pipe (or flute) playing with the child miming the actions, but the thought of all the technical things that could go wrong dissuaded me! Having an actor who can actually play the pipe or flute performing the role of the PIED PIPER would be ideal, but is quite unlikely. If you have someone else who can play the flute or a similar pipelike instrument, cueing him or her live to the actions of the actor is a possibility. Or, if you have time to rehearse it thoroughly, consider the option of using recorded music. In our production, it didn't matter that nothing was heard when the PIED PIPER played. The text implies that the Piper's music means different things to different characters, which gives you you 'artistic licence' to opt for silence! If you do choose live playing, make sure that it's impressive and 'magical'.

It is also interesting to use music as a character theme, playing the same tune each time a particular character enters. However, this should really only be attempted with one or two characters, and its use should be limited to avoid irritating the audience!

When you are choosing music, the obvious choices are usually the best; but if you have time, try to search for a song or piece of music which reflects the context or mood, rather than just picking up a general theme.

If you don't want your 'actors' to sing, other children in the school can be utilised as a chorus seated around the staging area; they can sing the songs while those on stage mime appropriate actions.

Don't forget to utilise your talented school musicians – both teachers and pupils! Music doesn't have to be 'tuneful' or played from musical scores to be effective. Interesting 'musical sound effects' can be created with a variety of unusual or home-made instruments. My big moment in a school production was providing the 'elephant' sounds on a baritone horn for a performance of *The Jungle Book*!

PROPS

Again, this play is very simple to stage. The only essential props are as follows:

- Large, old books for the NARRATORS to appear to read from. They can place their scripts inside.
- A small table and five small chairs for the MAYOR and CORPORATION (Scene 1).
- A pipe for the PIED PIPER. (We used a wooden recorder.)
- A walking stick or crutch for CHILD 6.
- A small bag of money for the Mayor to offer to the PIED PIPER (Scene 4).
- A large sign saying 'PIED PIPER'S STREET' (for use in Scene 6).

Nothing else is essential, though I'm sure your RATS would enjoy eating various 'food props'. This would look effective, but could be a nightmare in terms of clearing all debris from the stage! Papers and files could also be used to litter the table during the council meeting in Scene 1.

However, the essential point to remember with **all** props is: 'If it goes on, it must come off.' If a prop makes its way **onto** the stage, then it must somehow make its way **off** again! Actors (of all ages) are notoriously bad at remembering this.

COSTUMES

The 'wardrobe' for *The Pied Piper of Hamelin* can be fairly simple to organize, though you will need to spend some time making or finding suitable costumes for some of the characters. If you have the time and skill to create wonderfully elaborate costumes, then feel free to do so! If not, the following ideas worked perfectly well for our production:

Narrators: These should be dressed in their own (smart) clothes. It is best to stipulate a colour scheme – either black and white, red and black, or similar. This will mean that they are wearing some form of recognizable 'costume' – and, more importantly, that they **feel** they are doing so. Narrators need the thrill of dressing up too!

Townspeople: Dress these in a generic 'fairy tale' costume, avoiding modern dress if at all possible. The aim is to create an 'olde worlde' village look. Dress females in long, flowing skirts with colourful shirts or blouses, aprons, headscarves and flat pumps. Dress males in smart trousers (not jeans), checked or coloured shirts, waistcoats, hats or caps and flat pumps or smart shoes. (Alternatively, all the TOWNSPEOPLE could be barefoot.)

Mayor: Dress him in smart black trousers and a smart white shirt with a bow tie. Cover this with a plush, full-length 'Mayor's robe' which fastens at the front, complete with a train if possible. He must wear smart black shoes or black pumps – not trainers! The MAYOR's fat stomach can be created by tucking a cushion down his trousers and up underneath his shirt (which will hold it in position). Our MAYOR's chain was made from gold ribbon with shapes cut from gold card threaded onto it, and looked very effective.

If you have time to create an elaborate robe and train for the MAYOR which clothes him entirely, he will only need to wear black leggings and a T-shirt underneath.

Corporation: Use exactly the same costume items as for the MAYOR, but without the train and the chain, and in less plush material. However, they must still look wealthy and self-important.

Pied Piper: Dress him in a combination of red and yellow, either with red leggings and a yellow top (or T-shirt) or vice versa. He should either be barefoot or wear red or yellow pumps. If you have the good fortune to find (as I did), or are able to make, a red and yellow checked coat, the PIPER can wear this over the leggings and top. The PIPER's scarf in our production was made using a piece of red fabric twisted together with a piece of yellow fabric; the pipe was tied on. The whole outfit was very simple, but very effective.

Visit your local charity shops – that's where I found both the yellow and red checked coat and the material for the scarf.

Rats: Dress these in leggings, jogging bottoms or tights and T-shirts, sweatshirts, thin jumpers or tops of a uniform colour. We had black RATS, brown RATS, grey RATS and white RATS. Keep their feet bare (cut the feet off the tights) to make sure that they can move around quickly and easily without endangering themselves. Heavy jumpers should not be worn, as they can cause children to overheat and even to faint.

Our rat ears were made from felt, using the same colours as the rats' costumes, and stuck onto thick card. A small extra flap was created at the bottom of each 'ear' to be tucked under an elasticated headband; the ear was kept in place with several hairgrips.

We made pointed rat noses from small cones of black card or strong paper. The nose was threaded with elastic to slip over the child's nose, and the elastic loop was strung around the back of the head. Whiskers were made by cutting bristles out of a paint brush and gluing them onto the noses (which was fiddly, but effective). Make sure to measure the children for size of nose and width of head before making the rats' noses.

Our rats' tails were an inspiration! Take a pair of tights (using the same colours as your RAT costumes) and cut them in half, so that you have two legs. Fill each leg completely with bubble wrap which has been rolled to 'rat-tail' size. Tuck the spare piece of tight fabric into the child's leggings, jogging bottoms or tights and pin it in place from the inside. Flap the T-shirt, sweatshirt or top over it to hide the join, and you have some excellent rat's tails!

Check all of these appendages after each rehearsal and each performance (if there is more than one), as some mending may be necessary. Make the children responsible for their own ears, noses and tails. Warn them that if these get lost or damaged, they will be expected to go on stage without – and mean it!

Children: Dress these in jeans, coloured trousers, dungarees, long skirts or dresses, with bright shirts, blouses or T-shirts. Boots, smart shoes, flat shoes or pumps (not trainers) should be worn on the feet. The male and female CHILDREN must be clearly differentiated, in true 'stereotypical' manner!

MAKE-UP

The use of make-up is dependent on the type of lighting used. If you are working under professional stage lights, then more make-up must be applied, as these lights remove colour and contour from the face. However, if you are working under school lights or strip lights, be careful to apply just enough make-up to define features and express character. Water-based make-up is best for whole-face or body coverage; grease-based make-up is best for eyes, cheeks and lips. Make sure to practise applying the make-up before the performance!

The make-up needed for *The Pied Piper of Hamelin* is quite simple, and very little is required. I would suggest the following:

Narrators: These should be made up with simple, light lipstick and eyeshadow (plus a light base or foundation, if they are working under professional stage lights). Try to prevent them from applying too much, as it isn't necessary. It's more important that they look clean, tidy and smart.

Townspeople: They all need a little bit of foundation all over the face, with blue eyeshadow and a touch of blusher. The females should also have a nice red or pink lipstick. If you want to give the males a bit of stubble, take a small, firm brush (a blusher brush works well), cover it with black make-up (a black grease stick or similar) and tap it lightly end-on onto the face. Get the child to suck his or her lips in and apply just below the nose as well. Children will complain while it's being applied, but they love the effect. The main problem then is how to prevent them touching and smudging it!

Mayor: Use a light base of foundation, blue eyeshadow and pale red lips. Add rosy cheeks and a red-tipped nose (the result of all that eating and drinking). Age lines could be used to contour and define the face (see page 46), but these are not strictly necessary. The eyebrows can be darkened or thickened using a black grease stick or eyeliner pencil – this gives the character a slightly 'mad', sinister air, which is very effective.

Corporation: Use the same base as for the MAYOR, adding the rosy cheeks but not necessarily the red nose. Leave the eyebrows alone, but draw on curly moustaches using a black eyeliner pencil. This takes practice but can be very effective, and the children love them! None of these characters should have facial stubble, though the children will probably try to persuade you otherwise!

Pied Piper: A very simple, light foundation, combined with blue eyeshadow and pale red lips, is all that is needed. If you want to give the child a 'swarthy' complexion, suitable water-based make-up is available in a range of skin tones. However, if you decide to do this, remember that **every bit** of visible skin must be covered! The eyes can be defined using a black eyeliner pencil – this can be extended from the eyelid to give the character a slightly 'oriental' appearance if you wish. However, strong make-up is completely unnecessary for this character.

Rats: No make-up at all is needed, though you can use water-based all-over make-up to provide cover if you wish. This is available in all the colours you'll need for the RATS – but again, remember that once you start, every bit of visible flesh has to be covered!

Children: Keep it very simple, using basic foundation, blue eyeshadow, a little bit of blusher and a touch of pink or pale red lipstick. Boys may complain about the eye and mouth make-up, but they will need it to prevent their features from disappearing under the lights.

If you want to 'age' any characters, use a red-toned grease stick and a cocktail stick. Ask the children to screw up their faces and apply the grease paint to the wrinkles, using the cocktail stick. Think carefully about where wrinkles form on the face as you age, and draw them accordingly. However, be careful not to draw in too many lines, or the poor child will end up with a face like a road map!

LEARNING LINES

Children never fail to amaze me with their capacity for learning and retaining lines. However, everyone needs support in learning lines at some time. Methods that can help include the following:

REPETITION
This requires frequent and regular reading of the script. Go over the children's lines again and again, and they will learn them by rote. This method means that children often learn everyone else's lines as well –

which is not a problem unless they start prompting while on stage.

FROM CUES
Read the line immediately before a child's. Let the child read his or her line out loud. Read the 'cue line' again, but this time cover up the child's line on the script. This way, the children are learning the important cues as well as their own lines.

ON PAPER
Write each child's cue lines and own lines on a separate piece of paper, to prevent the children being daunted by a large script. Use this method for children to learn one scene or short section at a time. They can carry the pieces of paper around with them, and will memorize the lines quite quickly through absorbing these short extracts.

ON TAPE
Help the children to read through the script two or three times. Record each child's cue lines on tape, leaving a long pause after each one for the child to interject his or her own lines. Work through this with each child initially, using the script as an accompanying visual aid; then let the children try it alone. Gradually remove their dependence on using the script, until they can say their lines in the recorded pauses without hesitating. Alternatively, you could record both the cue lines and the child's own lines, then leave a gap for the child to repeat his or her own lines.

VERBAL SUPPORT
Some children find it easier to learn lines through hearing them spoken and simply repeating them. However, this can take up an awful lot of your rehearsal time!

In addition, enlist the support of family members to help the children with their lines. Encourage children to 'test' each other, and try to create an atmosphere of support. Don't be too worried if the children paraphrase their lines, as long as important aspects are not omitted.

Use what literacy time you can spare to read through the script a number of times as a whole group. Take a balanced approach: emphasize that the children need to remember what they will say, but don't frighten them so much that they forget everything!

It is up to you whether or not you appoint a designated 'prompter' for the performances. I prefer not to use one, as the children can end up relying too much on being fed lines and not on their own ability to learn them. If you decide to have one, your prompter should attend **all** of the rehearsals, in order to make sure that he or she is thoroughly familiar with the performance.

CALMING NERVES AND CHANNELLING ENERGY

Those children who become stressed and nervous about performing must be allowed to feel that they have a 'get-out clause'. If possible, have another child in mind who can take over their lines, and let them know that they don't **have** to perform if they really don't want to. I say this on a regular basis to the young children I direct; and however terrified they may become, they always end up performing. I think this is because they know that taking part in the play is **their** choice, and that they can pull out at any time if they really want to.

Give the more 'energetic' (a euphemism for 'disruptive') children specific tasks to perform. I often involve these children in helping others to learn lines, in making props and even in applying make-up during rehearsals. Having a sense of responsibility about an important job will usually calm over-excited children. However, there is always the option of threatening to remove them from the play – and meaning it – if they don't calm down!

The trick is to keep all the children occupied. This prevents them from having time to be worried, and uses up spare energy. Use your rehearsal planning time to set up two or three production-related tasks that can be done while the rehearsals are in progress. Alternatively, bring drawing paper and crayons to rehearsals and ask children to draw the stage and set. I've also used word puzzles and colouring books, and asked children to write and decorate invitations for their families to come and see the play. All obvious strategies, but they work!

CURTAIN CALLS

I've seen some terrible curtain calls which have completely spoilt an otherwise good performance. Please bear in mind that this is the last memory your audience will have of the play, and that any sloppiness at this point will override the professionalism that may have gone before.

I'm not in favour of the pantomime-style 'walkdown' curtain call, where the actors come on to take their bows one by one to different audience responses. In fact, I'm completely against them. It must feel awful to act your heart out and then come on to a lukewarm reception when your co-actor has just received a rousing, foot-stamping cheer.

I prefer to structure my curtain calls as follows:

1. Line up all the children on stage in several rows according to height, with the tallest ones at the back. Space them out so they can all be seen.
2. Tell the children to look around and notice who they are standing next to, in front of and behind.
3. Tell all the children to stand upright, with their feet together and their hands resting lightly on the front of their thighs.
4. Now nominate one child in the centre of the front row to start the bow. Tell all the other children to watch this child carefully, without making their observation noticeable.
5. When the nominated child on the front row bows slowly, everyone must bow. Bowing should be done from the waist, with the hands sliding down to the knees and the eyes directed at the floor. Make sure that everyone moves at the same, slow pace: bowing too quickly can give the appearance of a group of nodding ducks!
6. Tell the children to hold the bowing position for a slow count of 'two'; then everyone should straighten up again.
7. Repeat, with everyone following the front row leader.

That is all that's required!

Finally, make sure that the children maintain the same level of professionalism when leaving the stage. Don't allow them to scream, shout, wave to their Mums or whatever. A smooth, professional ending can really round off a lovely performance.

LITERACY SUPPORT

The following are some brief suggestions for literacy activities that could follow on from reading and performing the playscript.

STORY

● Write an additional scene for the play, continuing the story in playscript form and using the same style as the author.
● Devise an alternative ending for the play and improvise a script before recording it in writing or on tape.
● Write about the events of the play in the style of a newspaper reporter.

CHARACTERS

● Perform the play using simple puppets, paying particular attention to the voices for the different characters and the Narrators.
● Write a description of your favourite character, choosing suitable adjectives to describe his or her appearance and personality.
● Write the play as a story told from the perspective of one of the characters.

THEME

● Decide as a class what you think the main theme of the play is. In small groups, improvise and then write a short play based on the same theme. The groups can perform their plays to the rest of the class.

● Explore and discuss what action the Pied Piper took when the Mayor refused to pay him. Explain the problem and suggest alternative courses of action. Evaluate the advice offered by the writer at the very end of the play: *...if we've promised them aught, let us keep our promise!*

WORKING WITH THE PLAYSCRIPT

● Explore the layout conventions for playscripts, using a short section of the text. Look at how stage directions are written, how the scenes are structured, and so on. Explain these conventions in writing.
● Devise a 'Glossary of Terms' to accompany the play, defining difficult or obscure words and phrases.
● Explore the use of **similes** in the rhyming narrative. Invent alternative similes of your own.

PERFORMANCE-RELATED TASKS

● Write and design a programme for the play which gives the audience all the relevant information.
● Design and draw a set for the play. Explain and justify your design in writing.